PRINCEWILL LAGANG

Reigniting Desire: Overcoming Relationship Ruts

First published by PRINCEWILL LAGANG 2023

Copyright © 2023 by Princewill Lagang

All rights reserved. No part of this publication may be reproduced, stored or transmitted in any form or by any means, electronic, mechanical, photocopying, recording, scanning, or otherwise without written permission from the publisher. It is illegal to copy this book, post it to a website, or distribute it by any other means without permission.

Princewill Lagang asserts the moral right to be identified as the author of this work.

First edition

This book was professionally typeset on Reedsy.
Find out more at reedsy.com

Contents

1. Introduction — 1
2. Recognizing Relationship Ruts — 4
3. Understanding the Impact — 7
4. Rediscovering Passion — 10
5. Communication Breakdown — 13
6. Navigating Routine and Monotony — 16
7. Embracing Change Together — 19
8. Prioritizing Intimacy — 22
9. Self-Exploration and Self-Care — 25
10. Reinventing Date Nights — 28
11. Addressing Unresolved Issues — 31
12. Sustaining a Renewed Relationship — 34

1

Introduction

In the intricate landscape of human relationships, the concept of "relationship ruts" stands as a common phenomenon that often goes unnoticed until it becomes a formidable obstacle. These ruts, characterized by a sense of stagnation, routine, and diminishing desire, can significantly impact the vibrancy and longevity of a partnership. This chapter delves into the intricacies of relationship ruts and highlights the crucial importance of addressing these challenges to foster a thriving and enduring partnership.

Section 1.1: Unveiling Relationship Ruts

At the heart of every romantic relationship lies a delicate balance between familiarity and novelty. As the initial excitement of a partnership evolves into a more settled phase, couples may find themselves ensnared in a rhythm of predictability. This rhythm, while offering comfort and stability, can inadvertently give rise to relationship ruts. These ruts manifest in various ways - from dwindling communication and diminished physical intimacy to a growing sense of emotional distance. By examining the nuances of these ruts, we can gain a deeper understanding of the factors that contribute to their emergence.

Section 1.2: The Erosion of Desire

A hallmark of relationship ruts is the erosion of desire. What was once a burning passion gradually gives way to a tepid sense of duty or routine. The intense longing to connect with a partner physically and emotionally can be smothered by the pressures of daily life, leaving couples grappling with a void that cannot be ignored. By exploring the psychological underpinnings of desire and the dynamics that govern its trajectory, we can shed light on the mechanics of desire's decline within the context of relationship ruts.

Section 1.3: Navigating the Complexities

As couples navigate the evolving landscape of their partnership, it becomes imperative to confront the challenges posed by relationship ruts. Ignoring or neglecting these challenges can lead to a gradual deterioration of the relationship's core, leaving both partners feeling unfulfilled and disconnected. This section underscores the significance of acknowledging the existence of ruts and the role they play in shaping the trajectory of a relationship. By doing so, couples can initiate a proactive and purposeful journey towards rejuvenation.

Section 1.4: The Road to a Thriving Partnership

While relationship ruts pose a significant threat, they also offer an opportunity for growth and transformation. Addressing these challenges head-on requires a commitment to open communication, self-awareness, and shared efforts. Couples who recognize the importance of maintaining desire and intimacy in their relationship can embark on a journey to reignite the spark that initially brought them together. This chapter sets the stage for a comprehensive exploration of strategies, insights, and practical approaches to overcome relationship ruts and cultivate a partnership that thrives amidst the complexities of modern life.

In summary, this introductory chapter lays the foundation for a comprehensive examination of the phenomenon of relationship ruts and their impact on desire within a partnership. By acknowledging the existence of these

INTRODUCTION

challenges and their implications, couples can pave the way for a more fulfilling and enduring relationship journey.

2

Recognizing Relationship Ruts

In the intricate landscape of romantic partnerships, recognizing the presence of relationship ruts is a pivotal step towards fostering a healthier and more vibrant connection. This chapter delves into the nuanced understanding of relationship ruts, defines their various manifestations, and provides insights into how individuals can identify when their relationship might be ensnared in a rut.

Section 2.1: Defining Relationship Ruts

Relationship ruts can be understood as periods of stagnation, monotony, and diminished emotional connection within a romantic partnership. These ruts emerge when the initial excitement and novelty of a relationship transition into a phase of routine and predictability. They are characterized by a decline in various aspects of the partnership, including communication, intimacy, and shared activities. By understanding the core attributes of relationship ruts, individuals can begin to unravel their complexities and address their implications.

Section 2.2: Manifestations of Relationship Ruts

Relationship ruts can manifest in a myriad of ways, often disguising themselves within the fabric of daily life. These manifestations encompass emotional, physical, and communicative dimensions of the relationship. Emotional manifestations might include a sense of emotional distance, lack of excitement, or complacency. Physical manifestations may entail a decrease in physical intimacy, decreased affection, or lack of sexual desire. Communication, a cornerstone of healthy relationships, can suffer in ruts, leading to miscommunication, lack of deep conversations, and emotional disconnection.

Section 2.3: Identifying Signs of Rut

Recognizing when a relationship is entrenched in a rut can be challenging, as these signs can be subtle and easily overlooked. One prominent indicator is a persistent feeling of discontent or unease, often accompanied by a sense of longing for past times when the relationship felt more invigorating. Changes in communication patterns, such as a decline in meaningful conversations or a reliance on superficial exchanges, can also signal a potential rut. Additionally, a noticeable decrease in physical intimacy, coupled with a lack of excitement about spending time together, may indicate that the relationship is losing its spark.

Section 2.4: Self-Reflection and Open Dialogue

Identifying relationship ruts necessitates a combination of self-reflection and open dialogue between partners. Individuals should engage in introspection to assess their own feelings and desires within the partnership. Open and honest conversations between partners are crucial in this process. Sharing feelings of dissatisfaction, discussing unmet needs, and collectively acknowledging the presence of a rut can serve as the first step toward overcoming its effects.

Section 2.5: Seeking Professional Guidance

In cases where identifying and addressing relationship ruts becomes challenging, seeking professional guidance from relationship counselors or therapists can be immensely beneficial. These professionals offer an external perspective and a wealth of strategies to help couples navigate the complexities of relationship ruts and emerge stronger.

In conclusion, Chapter 2 has provided an in-depth understanding of relationship ruts, their various manifestations, and the telltale signs that a partnership might be ensnared in one. By recognizing these signs and addressing them through self-awareness, open communication, and, when necessary, seeking professional guidance, couples can embark on a journey towards revitalizing their relationship and fostering a renewed sense of connection and desire.

3

Understanding the Impact

Within the intricate web of romantic relationships, the effects of relationship ruts ripple far beyond the surface, touching the very core of desire, intimacy, and emotional well-being. This chapter delves into the profound implications of relationship ruts on these aspects, shedding light on the erosion of passion and the potential consequences for the emotional well-being of both partners.

Section 3.1: Erosion of Desire and Intimacy

At the heart of any passionate partnership lies the delicate interplay between desire and intimacy. Relationship ruts pose a significant threat to these essential elements, often leading to a gradual erosion of the intense longing and emotional closeness that were once the bedrock of the relationship. As routine takes over and excitement wanes, couples find themselves grappling with a diminished desire for physical and emotional connection. Intimacy becomes mechanical, and the spark that once ignited their bond begins to flicker, leaving a void that is difficult to ignore.

Section 3.2: Emotional Consequences

The toll of relationship ruts extends beyond physical aspects, reaching into the realm of emotional well-being. As desire diminishes and intimacy fades, partners may begin to experience a wide range of negative emotions. Frustration, resentment, and loneliness can set in as the partnership loses its vibrancy. The lack of emotional connection can lead to feelings of isolation and a sense of unfulfillment. These emotions, left unaddressed, can fester and contribute to a growing emotional distance between partners.

Section 3.3: Self-Esteem and Identity

The impact of relationship ruts is not limited to the relationship itself; it can also affect individual self-esteem and identity. When a partner perceives a decline in desire or intimacy, they might question their attractiveness or worthiness. This self-doubt can seep into various aspects of their life, affecting their confidence and overall well-being. Similarly, the partnership's stagnation can hinder personal growth and the pursuit of individual passions, as partners become entrenched in the rut's dynamics.

Section 3.4: Communication Breakdown

A significant consequence of relationship ruts is the breakdown of communication. As the partnership loses its dynamism, conversations can become superficial and transactional, lacking the depth and vulnerability that are essential for a healthy relationship. The inability to openly discuss feelings, desires, and concerns can exacerbate the effects of relationship ruts, perpetuating a cycle of disconnection.

Section 3.5: Navigating Emotional Challenges

Recognizing the emotional consequences of relationship ruts is a crucial step toward addressing their impact. Partners must engage in open and honest conversations about their feelings, desires, and concerns. This proactive approach can help alleviate negative emotions and foster a renewed sense of understanding and empathy.

In conclusion, Chapter 3 has illuminated the multifaceted impact of relationship ruts on desire, intimacy, and emotional well-being. By understanding these consequences, couples can appreciate the urgency of addressing relationship ruts and the importance of proactive measures to reignite the spark of passion, reconnect emotionally, and cultivate a relationship that thrives on mutual understanding and shared growth.

4

Rediscovering Passion

Passion, the lifeblood of a vibrant relationship, holds the power to rejuvenate, connect, and infuse intimacy into the partnership. This chapter delves into the pivotal role of passion in sustaining a thriving relationship, examines the factors that contribute to its gradual fade, and provides insights into how couples can reignite the flames of passion and restore the vitality of their connection.

Section 4.1: The Significance of Passion

Passion serves as the driving force that propels a relationship beyond the mundane and into the realm of emotional and physical intimacy. It fuels excitement, fosters a sense of deep connection, and contributes to the overall health and longevity of the partnership. The palpable energy that passion brings can dissolve the barriers of routine and complacency, allowing partners to continuously explore and rediscover each other.

Section 4.2: The Fade of Passion

Despite its initial intensity, passion often experiences a gradual decline as relationships progress. The exhilaration of newness gives way to familiarity, and partners can find themselves caught in the routines of everyday life. External stresses, such as work pressures and family commitments, can consume time and energy, leaving little room for nurturing passion. Moreover, a lack of intentional effort to sustain passion can lead to its erosion over time.

Section 4.3: Reigniting the Flames

The path to reigniting passion requires deliberate and conscious actions from both partners. Communication serves as a cornerstone, as discussing desires, fantasies, and preferences can open doors to new experiences. Engaging in shared activities that spark joy and excitement can rekindle the sense of adventure that was once abundant in the relationship. Exploring new facets of intimacy, both emotional and physical, can create an environment conducive to passion's revival.

Section 4.4: Cultivating Novelty and Spontaneity

Novelty and spontaneity are potent antidotes to the monotony that accompanies relationship ruts. Partners can inject freshness into their connection by trying new things together, whether it's embarking on an adventure, exploring a shared interest, or surprising each other with thoughtful gestures. By breaking away from the predictable routine, couples create opportunities for passion to flourish.

Section 4.5: Prioritizing Intimacy and Connection

Intimacy is the fertile ground from which passion blossoms. Fostering emotional intimacy through deep conversations, active listening, and vulnerability can pave the way for a resurgence of passion. Equally important is physical intimacy, where partners prioritize their connection through touch, affection, and sexual exploration. Intimacy and passion are closely intertwined; nurturing one naturally enhances the other.

In conclusion, Chapter 4 has underscored the pivotal role of passion in maintaining a vibrant relationship. It has explored the reasons behind its fading and provided practical insights into how couples can reignite the flames of passion. By acknowledging the importance of passion, intentionally cultivating novelty, and prioritizing intimacy and connection, couples can navigate the challenges of relationship ruts and embark on a journey of rediscovery that leads to a renewed sense of excitement, intimacy, and fulfillment.

5

Communication Breakdown

Communication, the cornerstone of any successful relationship, can either be a powerful tool for connection or a harbinger of disconnection. This chapter delves into the role of communication breakdown in exacerbating relationship ruts, explores how it contributes to emotional distance, and offers strategies for effective communication to bridge gaps and foster a renewed sense of intimacy.

Section 5.1: The Impact of Communication Breakdown

Communication breakdown is a key catalyst in the emergence of relationship ruts. As partners become entrenched in routines and familiarity, conversations often shift from meaningful exchanges to superficial chit-chat. The lack of deep communication robs the partnership of the emotional intimacy required to sustain passion and connection. Misunderstandings can escalate due to assumptions, leading to resentment and emotional distance.

Section 5.2: Emotional Distance and Assumptions

In the absence of open communication, emotional distance can take root. Partners may start assuming each other's thoughts, feelings, and intentions, leading to misunderstandings that further fuel the disconnection.

Unaddressed concerns or unspoken desires can fester, contributing to a sense of dissatisfaction and complacency. Emotional walls are erected, hindering vulnerability and genuine connection.

Section 5.3: Strategies for Effective Communication

To combat the damaging effects of communication breakdown, couples must actively work on enhancing their communication skills. This involves prioritizing open and honest dialogues that delve into both the light and the shadow aspects of the relationship. Strategies include:

1. Active Listening: Paying full attention to your partner's words and non-verbal cues, validating their feelings, and showing empathy.

2. Vulnerability: Sharing fears, desires, and concerns openly, fostering an environment where both partners feel safe to express themselves authentically.

3. Regular Check-Ins: Setting aside dedicated time for meaningful conversations to discuss the state of the relationship, individual needs, and shared goals.

4. Non-Defensive Communication: Avoiding blame and defensiveness when discussing sensitive topics, focusing on understanding rather than winning an argument.

5. Clarification: Asking questions to ensure mutual understanding, preventing assumptions from snowballing into larger misunderstandings.

Section 5.4: Cultivating Emotional Intelligence

Emotional intelligence plays a pivotal role in effective communication. Partners should strive to understand and manage their own emotions, as well as those of their significant other. Recognizing emotional triggers and learning how to navigate them with empathy can prevent conflicts from escalating and deepen the emotional connection.

Section 5.5: Seeking Professional Guidance

In cases where communication breakdown persists, seeking professional help, such as couples therapy or counseling, can be invaluable. A trained professional can guide partners in improving their communication skills, breaking down barriers, and finding constructive ways to address their challenges.

In conclusion, Chapter 5 has illuminated the detrimental impact of communication breakdown on relationships, particularly in the context of relationship ruts. By recognizing the role of effective communication as a bridge to intimacy, employing strategies for open dialogues, and fostering emotional intelligence, couples can transcend the barriers of disconnection, reignite passion, and cultivate a partnership that thrives on mutual understanding and connection.

6

Navigating Routine and Monotony

Routine and monotony, while providing a sense of stability, can unwittingly sap the vibrancy from a romantic relationship. This chapter delves into the ways in which routine and monotony contribute to decreased desire, explores their impact on emotional intimacy, and provides an array of creative strategies to inject excitement and novelty, rekindling the spark that sustains passion.

Section 6.1: The Perils of Routine and Monotony

Routine and monotony can have a profound impact on a relationship's vitality. As partners settle into a predictable rhythm, the excitement that once accompanied novelty can wane, leading to a gradual decrease in desire. The predictability of everyday life can overshadow the sense of adventure and exploration that initially characterized the partnership. As a result, couples may find themselves feeling disconnected, emotionally distant, and less inclined to engage in intimate interactions.

Section 6.2: Diminished Desire and Emotional Connection

The erosion of desire is intricately linked to the stagnation that accompanies routine and monotony. Partners may become more focused on responsibilities, chores, and obligations, leaving little room for spontaneous expressions of affection or shared moments of joy. The lack of novelty and excitement can lead to emotional detachment, leaving partners yearning for the emotional connection that once fueled their passion.

Section 6.3: Infusing Excitement and Novelty

Breaking free from the clutches of routine requires a deliberate commitment to infusing excitement and novelty into the relationship. Creative strategies include:

1. Exploring New Activities: Engaging in activities that both partners haven't experienced before can ignite a sense of shared adventure.

2. Surprise Gestures: Spontaneous acts of kindness, surprise gifts, or planned date nights can inject a fresh spark of excitement.

3. Travel and Exploration: Planning trips, whether short getaways or exotic vacations, offers opportunities for new experiences and shared memories.

4. Role Play and Fantasy: Exploring role-playing or sharing fantasies can introduce an element of excitement into the bedroom.

5. Learning Together: Enrolling in a class or pursuing a new hobby as a couple fosters a sense of growth and shared interest.

6. Rekindling Old Traditions: Reviving past traditions or creating new ones can add a layer of anticipation and excitement to the relationship.

Section 6.4: Embracing Spontaneity

Embracing spontaneity involves breaking away from rigid routines and allowing room for unexpected experiences. Partners can surprise each other with impromptu outings, unplanned activities, or last-minute adventures. Embracing spontaneity encourages partners to be present in the moment, fostering a sense of shared excitement and emotional connection.

Section 6.5: Continuous Exploration

Novelty and excitement are not isolated events; they are ongoing pursuits. Couples must be committed to continuously exploring new facets of each other and their relationship. Regularly brainstorming new ideas, setting goals for shared adventures, and fostering an attitude of curiosity can keep the flame of passion alive.

In conclusion, Chapter 6 has illuminated the detrimental impact of routine and monotony on desire and emotional intimacy. By recognizing the need for excitement and novelty, embracing spontaneity, and committing to continuous exploration, couples can navigate the challenges posed by routine and monotony. Through these efforts, they can breathe new life into their partnership, reignite passion, and create a relationship that thrives on shared experiences, growth, and mutual fulfillment.

7

Embracing Change Together

The only constant in life is change, and navigating these transitions as a united team is essential for maintaining desire, intimacy, and the health of a romantic relationship. This chapter delves into the ways in which life changes can impact desire and emotional intimacy, explores the challenges they bring, and offers strategies for couples to navigate these shifts while fostering a strong and enduring connection.

Section 7.1: The Impact of Life Changes

Life changes, whether they be career shifts, moving to a new place, becoming parents, or facing personal challenges, can have a profound impact on desire and intimacy. These transitions often disrupt routines and dynamics, creating stressors that can strain emotional and physical connections. The shift in priorities and responsibilities can lead to emotional distance, as partners navigate their own adjustments individually.

Section 7.2: Challenges and Opportunities

While life changes pose challenges, they also present opportunities for growth and renewal within the relationship. By addressing the challenges as a united front, partners can cultivate a deeper sense of connection and understanding. Viewing life changes as a chance to learn, adapt, and evolve together can create a foundation for tackling challenges hand in hand.

Section 7.3: Effective Communication During Transitions

Clear and open communication is crucial when facing life changes. Partners should engage in honest conversations about their fears, hopes, and expectations. Sharing concerns and discussing how the changes might impact their desire and intimacy can help prevent misunderstandings and mitigate emotional distance.

Section 7.4: Prioritizing Quality Time

Amidst life changes, it's easy to let quality time slip through the cracks. However, making intentional efforts to spend quality time together is paramount. Partners can schedule regular date nights, engage in shared activities, or simply set aside moments to connect and check in with each other.

Section 7.5: Adapting Intimacy

Life changes often require adjustments to intimacy, both emotional and physical. Partners can openly discuss their needs and desires, exploring ways to continue fostering emotional connection even when faced with time constraints. Flexibility and understanding are key as couples adapt their physical intimacy to accommodate changing circumstances.

Section 7.6: Teamwork and Mutual Support

Embracing change as a united team is the cornerstone of navigating transitions successfully. Partners can provide mutual support by actively listening, validating each other's feelings, and collaborating on solutions. Viewing themselves as allies rather than adversaries allows them to tackle challenges with resilience and unity.

Section 7.7: Seeking Professional Guidance

In cases where life changes create significant strain, seeking professional help, such as couples counseling, can provide valuable tools for coping and adapting. A therapist can offer guidance on effective communication, conflict resolution, and strategies for maintaining intimacy during times of change.

In conclusion, Chapter 7 has highlighted the impact of life changes on desire and intimacy within a relationship. By approaching these transitions as opportunities for growth, practicing effective communication, prioritizing quality time, adapting intimacy, and fostering teamwork, couples can navigate challenges together and emerge from life changes with a strengthened bond. Embracing change as a shared journey allows partners to maintain desire, emotional connection, and the health of their partnership amidst the ebb and flow of life.

8

Prioritizing Intimacy

In the intricate dance of romantic relationships, the act of prioritizing intimacy becomes a beacon of hope, guiding partners through the challenges of ruts and fostering a renewed sense of connection. This chapter delves into the paramount importance of both physical and emotional intimacy in overcoming relationship ruts, and offers a repertoire of techniques to enhance connection, rekindle desire, and strengthen the bond between partners.

Section 8.1: The Vital Role of Intimacy

Intimacy serves as the glue that holds a romantic relationship together. Both physical and emotional intimacy are essential for bridging gaps, fostering connection, and reigniting the spark that diminishes in the face of ruts. Intimacy allows partners to share vulnerabilities, desires, and fears, creating a safe space for emotional growth and mutual understanding.

Section 8.2: Fostering Emotional Intimacy

Emotional intimacy involves open communication, empathy, and vulnerability. Partners can prioritize emotional connection by engaging in deep conversations, sharing their dreams and fears, and actively listening to each other's thoughts and feelings. Creating an environment where both partners feel understood and accepted is a foundational step toward overcoming ruts.

Section 8.3: Nurturing Physical Intimacy

Physical intimacy is a tangible expression of desire and connection. To nurture physical intimacy, couples should focus on touch, affection, and sexual exploration. Regular physical affection, such as hugging, holding hands, and kissing, can foster closeness. Additionally, exploring new ways to connect sexually can reignite desire and passion.

Section 8.4: Introducing Novelty

Novelty and spontaneity play a pivotal role in enhancing intimacy. Partners can inject excitement into their connection by trying new things together. This might involve exploring new places, engaging in novel activities, or even surprising each other with romantic gestures.

Section 8.5: Scheduling Intimacy

In the hustle and bustle of life, carving out time for intimacy is essential. Couples can benefit from scheduling "intimacy dates" where they dedicate time solely to connecting emotionally and physically. Setting aside this time signals the commitment to prioritizing intimacy in the relationship.

Section 8.6: Practicing Mindfulness

Mindfulness involves being fully present in the moment. Partners can practice mindfulness during shared experiences, conversations, and moments of intimacy. This practice deepens the connection by allowing partners to focus on each other without distractions, fostering a sense of presence and authenticity.

Section 8.7: Exploring Fantasies and Desires

Openly discussing fantasies, desires, and preferences can add a layer of excitement and novelty to the relationship. Partners can create an atmosphere of trust where they feel safe sharing their innermost thoughts, leading to a deeper understanding of each other's desires.

Section 8.8: Seeking Professional Guidance

In cases where intimacy challenges persist, seeking professional help from a therapist or counselor specializing in relationships can be beneficial. Professionals can guide partners in navigating barriers, addressing underlying issues, and developing strategies to enhance intimacy.

In conclusion, Chapter 8 has illuminated the integral role of intimacy in overcoming relationship ruts. By prioritizing both emotional and physical intimacy, introducing novelty, scheduling time for connection, practicing mindfulness, exploring desires, and seeking professional guidance when necessary, couples can bridge gaps, rekindle desire, and create a partnership that thrives on mutual understanding, passion, and fulfillment.

9

Self-Exploration and Self-Care

In the intricate tapestry of relationships, individual growth and self-care serve as the building blocks for revitalizing desire and reigniting the flame that might dim in the face of ruts. This chapter delves into the pivotal role of self-exploration and self-care in nurturing a thriving partnership, encouraging partners to invest in themselves as a means to enrich and deepen the connection they share.

Section 9.1: The Nexus of Individual Growth and Relationship Enrichment

The journey of self-exploration and self-care intertwines intimately with the health of a romantic relationship. Partners who invest in their personal growth and well-being contribute to the relationship's vitality. By nurturing their own passions, interests, and aspirations, individuals not only enrich their own lives but also bring renewed energy and vibrancy to the partnership.

Section 9.2: The Power of Self-Care

Self-care is a deliberate practice that involves prioritizing one's physical, emotional, and mental well-being. Partners who take the time to care for themselves are better equipped to navigate the challenges that relationship ruts present. Self-care provides a foundation of emotional resilience, allowing individuals to approach their partnership from a place of strength and authenticity.

Section 9.3: Rediscovering Personal Passions

As relationships progress, personal passions can sometimes take a backseat. Rediscovering and nurturing these passions can breathe new life into the partnership. Partners can encourage each other to pursue hobbies, interests, and goals that bring them joy and fulfillment. Sharing these aspects of themselves can lead to deeper understanding and connection.

Section 9.4: Embracing Growth and Change

Individual growth is an ongoing process that involves embracing change and embracing the opportunities for learning and development that life presents. Partners who actively seek personal growth inspire a culture of evolution within the relationship. As individuals evolve, they bring fresh perspectives, insights, and experiences to share with their partner.

Section 9.5: Nurturing Self-Esteem and Confidence

Self-exploration and self-care contribute to the cultivation of self-esteem and confidence. Partners who value and invest in themselves radiate a sense of self-assuredness that enhances the relationship. Confidence breeds open communication, vulnerability, and the willingness to explore new aspects of intimacy.

Section 9.6: Encouraging Partners to Invest in Themselves

Couples should encourage and support each other's efforts to engage in self-exploration and self-care. This involves recognizing and respecting each other's individual needs for growth, nurturing, and personal fulfillment. Partners can actively engage in conversations about their desires for personal development and the ways in which they envision supporting each other's journeys.

Section 9.7: Mutual Enrichment Through Individual Investment

By individually investing in growth and self-care, partners collectively enrich the relationship. The vibrancy and energy that arise from personal fulfillment spill over into the partnership, creating a positive feedback loop of mutual support and shared growth.

In conclusion, Chapter 9 has emphasized the profound impact of self-exploration and self-care on revitalizing desire and deepening the connection within a relationship. By prioritizing individual growth, rediscovering personal passions, embracing change, and nurturing self-esteem, partners can actively contribute to the thriving of their partnership. Encouraging each other to invest in themselves creates a dynamic foundation upon which desire, emotional intimacy, and mutual fulfillment can flourish amidst the complexities of life.

10

Reinventing Date Nights

Amidst the ebb and flow of life, date nights stand as an oasis of connection and rejuvenation in a romantic relationship. This chapter delves into the art of reinventing date nights, exploring the value of quality time for maintaining a strong bond, and offering a spectrum of creative ideas to refresh shared experiences, infuse novelty, and nurture the emotional and physical intimacy that sustains desire.

Section 10.1: The Essence of Quality Time

Date nights encapsulate the essence of quality time within a relationship. These moments allow partners to step away from the demands of daily life and immerse themselves in each other's company. Quality time is not merely a luxury; it is a precious investment in the foundation of the partnership.

Section 10.2: Breathing Life into Date Nights

To invigorate date nights and make them a source of excitement, partners should focus on infusing creativity, novelty, and shared experiences. The goal is to transcend routine and reignite the spark that might have faded amidst the challenges of daily life.

Section 10.3: Exploring New Environments

Stepping into new environments can spark curiosity and a sense of adventure. Partners can explore local attractions, visit museums, parks, or embark on spontaneous road trips to nearby destinations. The change of scenery can foster conversations and experiences that are fresh and engaging.

Section 10.4: Themed Evenings

Themed date nights add an element of fun and creativity. Partners can choose a theme - such as a movie night, a cuisine they've never tried, or even a retro-themed evening - and immerse themselves in the chosen theme for a memorable shared experience.

Section 10.5: Interactive Activities

Participating in interactive activities encourages engagement and playfulness. Options include cooking together, engaging in a paint and sip class, going to a trivia night, or even participating in an escape room challenge. These activities foster collaboration, laughter, and a sense of shared accomplishment.

Section 10.6: Outdoor Adventures

Nature provides an expansive canvas for rekindling connection. Partners can go hiking, have a picnic, go stargazing, or try their hand at a new outdoor sport. The beauty of the outdoors can encourage mindfulness and provide a backdrop for meaningful conversations.

Section 10.7: Nurturing Emotional Intimacy

Date nights also offer opportunities to nurture emotional intimacy. Partners can engage in deep conversations, reminisce about fond memories, and share dreams and aspirations. These moments of vulnerability and authenticity deepen the emotional connection.

Section 10.8: Making It a Regular Habit

Consistency is key to the impact of date nights. Partners should prioritize regular date nights to ensure a steady flow of quality time and connection. By scheduling these moments, couples send a clear message that their relationship remains a priority.

Section 10.9: Adjusting to Changing Circumstances

Life is dynamic, and circumstances can change. Partners should be adaptable in their approach to date nights, adjusting plans to accommodate different phases and challenges while still prioritizing their shared connection.

In conclusion, Chapter 10 has underscored the value of reinventing date nights as a vehicle for maintaining a strong bond within a relationship. By embracing creativity, exploring new environments, engaging in interactive activities, and nurturing emotional intimacy, couples can infuse their partnership with excitement, novelty, and shared experiences. Regular date nights serve as a testament to the enduring commitment of partners, fostering a relationship that thrives on mutual understanding, passion, and the joy of shared moments.

11

Addressing Unresolved Issues

Unresolved conflicts, like untended weeds, have the potential to choke the vibrancy out of a relationship, contributing to the emergence of ruts. This chapter delves into the ways in which unresolved issues can foster emotional distance and stagnation, explores their role in relationship ruts, and offers a toolkit of strategies for addressing and resolving these lingering conflicts to pave the way for renewed emotional connection and desire.

Section 11.1: The Silent Undercurrents

Unresolved issues act as silent undercurrents, subtly eroding the foundation of a partnership. When disagreements, misunderstandings, or hurtful incidents are left unaddressed, partners can feel distant, unheard, and resentful. The weight of these unresolved conflicts can contribute to emotional detachment and a decline in desire.

Section 11.2: The Role of Unresolved Conflicts in Ruts

Unresolved conflicts feed into the cycle of relationship ruts by perpetuating negative emotions and barriers to intimacy. Partners may become entangled in repetitive patterns of interaction, avoiding deep conversations out of fear of reigniting past conflicts. The emotional baggage from unresolved issues can cast a shadow over positive aspects of the relationship.

Section 11.3: Strategies for Addressing Unresolved Issues

Confronting unresolved conflicts requires courage, empathy, and a commitment to mutual growth. Strategies include:

1. Open Communication: Partners should initiate honest and non-confrontational conversations about the unresolved issues. Active listening, empathy, and validation are crucial in creating an environment where both parties feel heard.

2. Choose the Right Time and Place: Picking a suitable time and setting for these conversations is essential. Avoid discussing sensitive topics when emotions are running high or when external stressors are at their peak.

3. Focus on the Issue, Not the Person: Frame the discussion around the specific issue rather than blaming or criticizing each other. This approach helps keep the conversation constructive and prevents defensiveness.

4. Use "I" Statements: Express feelings and thoughts using "I" statements to convey personal experiences without assigning blame. This fosters understanding and minimizes defensiveness.

5. Seek Resolution, Not Victory: The goal of addressing unresolved conflicts is to find common ground and achieve resolution, rather than "winning" an argument. Partners should approach the conversation with a mindset of collaboration.

Section 11.4: Apologize and Forgive

Apologizing for one's role in the conflict and forgiving the other person are integral steps toward resolution. These acts of vulnerability and compassion help break down emotional barriers and pave the way for healing.

Section 11.5: Seek Compromise and Solutions

Partners should work together to find compromises and solutions that address the core issues. This collaborative approach ensures that both parties feel valued and that their needs are being acknowledged.

Section 11.6: Professional Mediation

In cases where conflicts are particularly entrenched or complex, seeking professional mediation through couples therapy or counseling can provide a structured and unbiased environment for addressing unresolved issues.

Section 11.7: Regular Check-Ins

To prevent the accumulation of unresolved conflicts, regular check-ins can be beneficial. Partners can engage in open discussions about their feelings, concerns, and needs, fostering ongoing understanding and connection.

In conclusion, Chapter 11 has shed light on the pivotal role of addressing unresolved issues in overcoming relationship ruts. By employing strategies such as open communication, choosing the right time and place, focusing on the issue, apologizing and forgiving, seeking compromise, and considering professional mediation when necessary, couples can untangle the knots of unresolved conflicts. By doing so, they pave the way for renewed emotional connection, rekindled desire, and a partnership that thrives on mutual growth and understanding.

12

Sustaining a Renewed Relationship

As partners traverse the journey of reigniting desire and overcoming the challenges of ruts, a renewed connection emerges, reminiscent of the early days of their relationship. This final chapter reflects on this transformative journey, summarizes key takeaways, and offers guidance for sustaining the rekindled emotional and physical intimacy that serves as the bedrock of their thriving partnership.

Section 12.1: The Journey of Transformation

The journey of reigniting desire and overcoming relationship ruts is a testament to the resilience, commitment, and love shared between partners. The dedication to understanding, growth, and connection has led to a transformation that goes beyond addressing challenges – it has breathed new life into the relationship.

Section 12.2: Embracing Change

Change is an integral part of any relationship. Partners must continue to embrace change as an opportunity for growth and renewal. Viewing life transitions as shared adventures that can strengthen their bond empowers couples to face challenges with unity and adaptability.

Section 12.3: Sustaining Intimacy

The sustenance of emotional and physical intimacy requires ongoing effort. Partners should remain vigilant in their commitment to open communication, quality time, and shared experiences. The strategies employed to reignite desire serve as the foundation for a sustained connection.

Section 12.4: Prioritizing Self-Care and Growth

As partners navigate the ebb and flow of life, prioritizing self-care and individual growth remains essential. Continuing to invest in personal passions and well-being enriches the relationship by bringing vibrancy and positive energy into the partnership.

Section 12.5: Navigating Conflicts

Conflicts are an inevitable part of relationships. However, the lessons learned in addressing and resolving conflicts during the journey of overcoming ruts should continue to be applied. Partners should remain committed to open communication, empathy, and compromise when navigating disagreements.

Section 12.6: Celebrating Milestones

Every step forward is a milestone worth celebrating. Partners should take the time to acknowledge and celebrate their achievements, whether they are small victories in communication or significant progress in addressing unresolved issues.

Section 12.7: Regular Reflection and Check-Ins

Reflection and check-ins should remain integral to the relationship. Partners can periodically revisit their progress, discuss their feelings and concerns, and recalibrate their strategies to ensure that they stay on the path of growth and connection.

Section 12.8: Seeking Professional Guidance

In moments of uncertainty or when facing new challenges, seeking professional guidance can provide valuable insights and tools. Couples therapy or counseling can serve as a safe space to navigate complexities and reinforce the strategies that have proven successful.

Section 12.9: Embracing the Ever-Evolving Journey

The journey of a relationship is ever-evolving, marked by twists, turns, and unexpected detours. Partners should approach this journey with a sense of curiosity, adaptability, and an unwavering commitment to each other's growth and happiness.

In summary, Chapter 12 reflects on the transformative journey undertaken by partners to reignite desire, overcome ruts, and cultivate a thriving partnership. By embracing change, sustaining intimacy, prioritizing self-care, navigating conflicts, celebrating milestones, and seeking professional guidance when needed, couples can ensure that their relationship remains dynamic, fulfilling, and characterized by a deep and lasting emotional and physical connection. The journey of sustaining a renewed relationship is one of ongoing growth, shared experiences, and the enduring power of love.

Conclusion: Navigating the Path to Lasting Desire and Intimacy

In the vast landscape of love, the journey to reignite desire and overcome the obstacles of relationship ruts stands as a testament to the indomitable spirit of human connection. Throughout the chapters of this guide, we have explored the intricacies of these challenges and delved into strategies to rekindle the emotional and physical intimacy that lie at the heart of a thriving partnership.

The transformative power of the journey is unmistakable. Partners who choose to face the complexities of their relationship head-on, who commit to open communication, vulnerability, and growth, find themselves on a path to renewal. By addressing communication breakdowns, nurturing emotional and physical intimacy, exploring new experiences, embracing change, and navigating unresolved conflicts, couples pave the way for a connection that transcends routine and stagnation.

The journey does not end here. The pages of this guide merely mark the beginning, a map to navigate through the terrain of love, growth, and renewal. The lessons learned and the strategies employed must become a part of the relationship's DNA. The commitment to each other's happiness, well-being, and fulfillment is a pact that should be upheld every day.

Relationships, much like the seasons, are in a constant state of change. Desire and intimacy, like a flame, require consistent fuel to burn brightly. The flame may flicker, but it need not fade. The key lies in prioritizing ongoing effort, nurturing emotional bonds, and fostering open communication. Reflecting on how far you've come and celebrating milestones serves as a reminder of the power of perseverance and dedication.

As you move forward, remember that love is not static; it's a dynamic force that evolves with you. The journey of lasting desire and intimacy is a tapestry woven with shared experiences, cherished moments, and a commitment to growth. Embrace the challenges as opportunities for deeper understanding and connection. Embrace change as a catalyst for renewal. Embrace communication as the lifeblood of your connection.

In the realm of relationships, the story is never truly written; it's an ongoing narrative filled with adventure, growth, and the resolute pursuit of happiness. The journey you've embarked upon to reignite desire and overcome ruts is not just a chapter but a testament to the strength of your bond. Keep writing your story with love, courage, and a shared commitment to lasting desire and intimacy.

www.ingramcontent.com/pod-product-compliance
Lightning Source LLC
LaVergne TN
LVHW010440070526
838199LV00066B/6116